JANET S. WONG

To Chloe—
Hooray for poetry
and you!

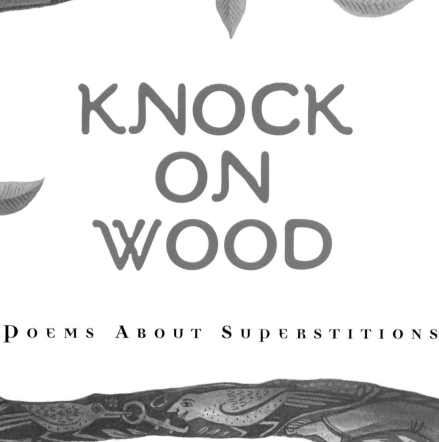

KNOCK ON WOOD

POEMS ABOUT SUPERSTITIONS

WRITTEN BY
janet s. wong

ILLUSTRATED BY
julie paschkis

Margaret K. McElderry Books

New York   London   Toronto   Sydney   Singapore

To Laura Kvasnosky
for showing me
Julie Paschkis's paintings
—J. W.

To Joe
—J. P.

Margaret K. McElderry Books

An imprint of Simon & Schuster Children's Publishing Division

1230 Avenue of the Americas, New York, New York 10020

Text copyright © 2003 by Janet S. Wong

Illustrations copyright © 2003 by Julianne Paschkis

All rights reserved, including the right of reproduction in whole or in part in any form.

Book design by Sonia Chaghatzbanian

The text for this book is set in Bliss.

The illustrations for this book are rendered in watercolors.

Manufactured in China

2 4 6 8 10 9 7 5 3 1

Library of Congress Cataloging-in-Publication Data

Wong, Janet S.

Knock on wood : poems about superstitions / Janet Wong ; illustrated by Julie Paschkis.

p. cm.

Summary: A collection of seventeen original poems about superstitions, including walking under a ladder,

breaking a mirror, and knocking on wood. Includes notes about the superstitions.

ISBN 0-689-85512-5

1. Superstition—Juvenile poetry. 2. Children's poetry, American.

[1. Superstition—Poetry. 2. American poetry.] I. Paschkis, Julie, ill. II. Title.

PS3573.O578 K58 2003

811'.54—dc21

2002008319

FIRST
EDITION

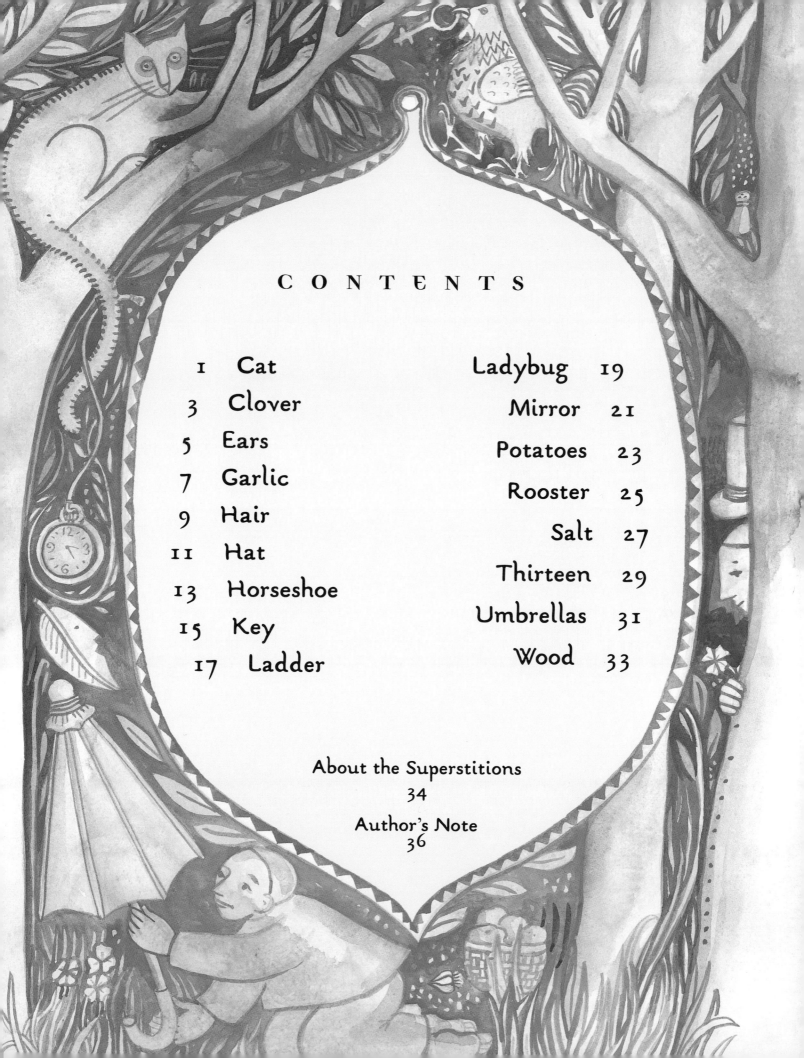

CONTENTS

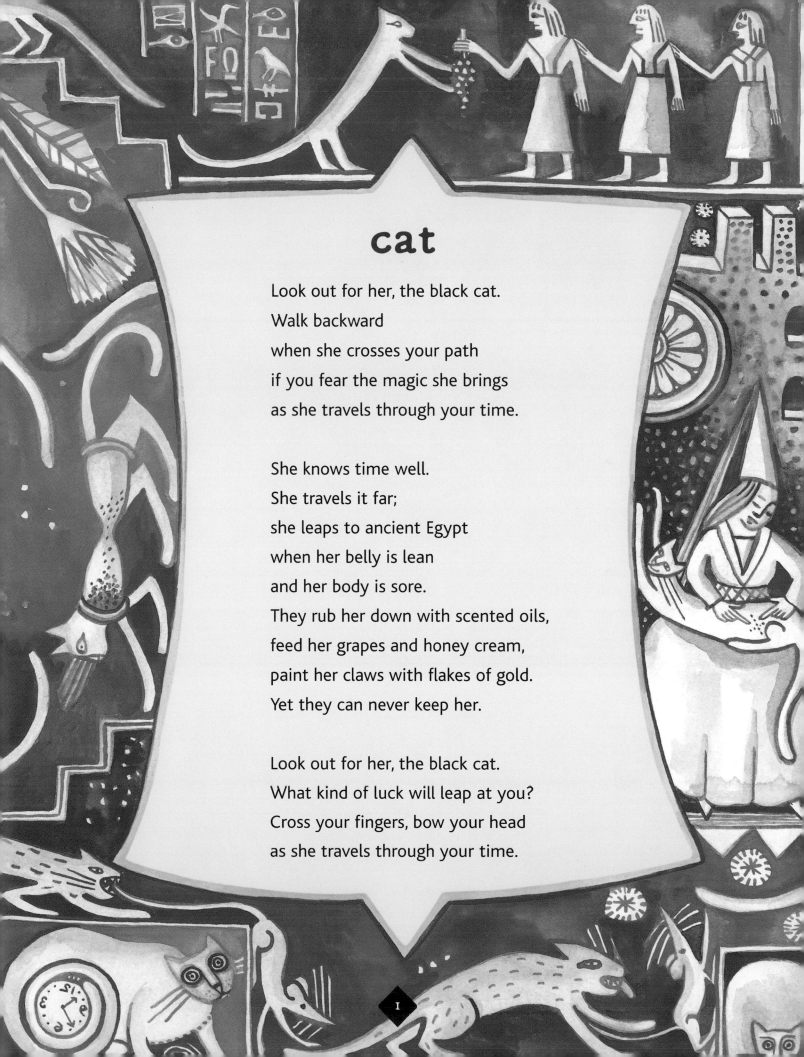

cat

Look out for her, the black cat.
Walk backward
when she crosses your path
if you fear the magic she brings
as she travels through your time.

She knows time well.
She travels it far;
she leaps to ancient Egypt
when her belly is lean
and her body is sore.
They rub her down with scented oils,
feed her grapes and honey cream,
paint her claws with flakes of gold.
Yet they can never keep her.

Look out for her, the black cat.
What kind of luck will leap at you?
Cross your fingers, bow your head
as she travels through your time.

clover

If you find a four-leaf clover in the grass,
you know a horse was born there
sometime.
In the days of fairies?

Fame, a faithful friend, wealth, good health.
These will be yours, doubled, they say—

if you give your clover to me.

ears

Your right ear itches? Let it be.
Someone talks about you now,
how kind you are, smart, how good.
Let it be, let songs be sung.

Your left ear itches? Pinch it quick.
Someone talks about you now,
how mean you are, dumb, how bad.
Pinch it, let him bite his tongue.

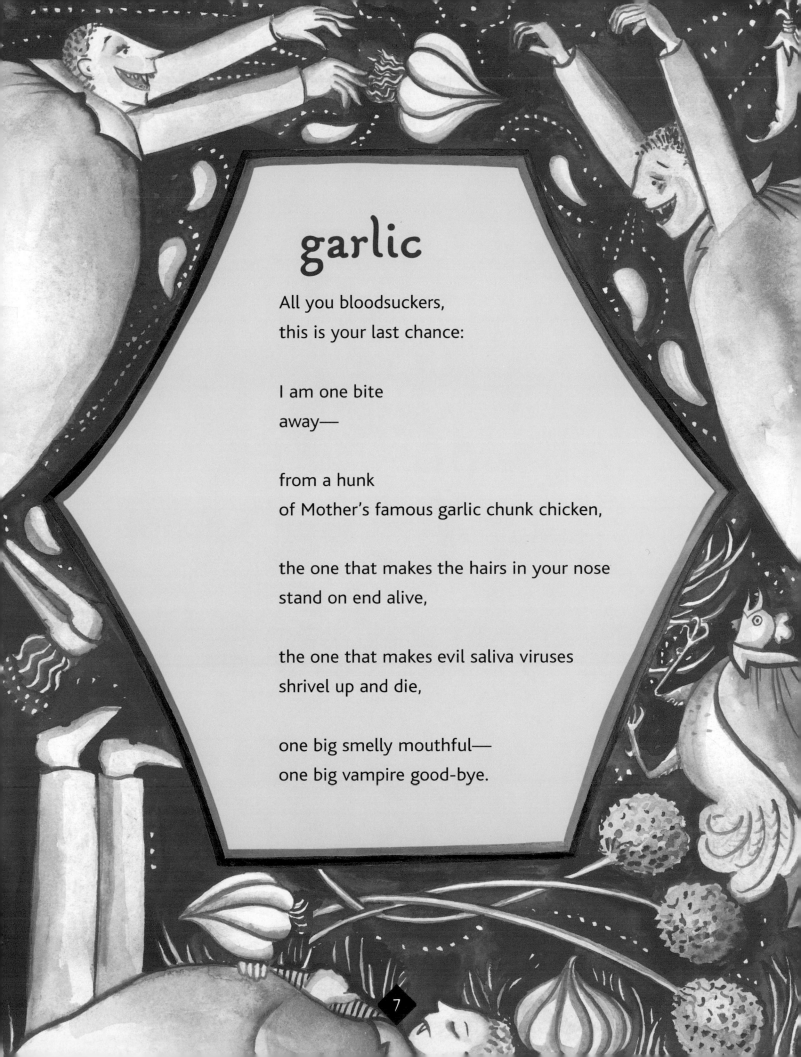

garlic

All you bloodsuckers,
this is your last chance:

I am one bite
away—

from a hunk
of Mother's famous garlic chunk chicken,

the one that makes the hairs in your nose
stand on end alive,

the one that makes evil saliva viruses
shrivel up and die,

one big smelly mouthful—
one big vampire good-bye.

hair

Eat the crust of fresh baked bread
for curly hair upon your head—

brush, don't comb, your hair at night,
and you won't hear a nasty fight—

Tuesday is your haircut day
if you want your luck to stay—

stand bareheaded in the rain
to cure a baldness in the brain.

hat

Don't put your hat on the table.
Don't put your hat on the bed.
Don't put your hat on backward, please,
and don't tell me now if you did—

but if you did, get a new one.
Don't try to fool your head.
Use your last dollar, borrow a dime,
and keep the luck on your lid.

horseshoe

Think of a horseshoe as a piggy bank of luck.
When you bring it home, hang it prongs up.
Then leave it to fill, full and rich,
with no one looking.

When it's time, the luck will spill.

key

Suppose you are walking along
and nowhere seems good enough.

You know those days.

Left. Right.
Which is the way?

Throw the keys over your shoulder.
The left one, go on.
Be sure there's no ditch,
no dog itching to grab and drop them
down a sewer drain.

Look.
The longest key points straight.

There
your surprise waits.

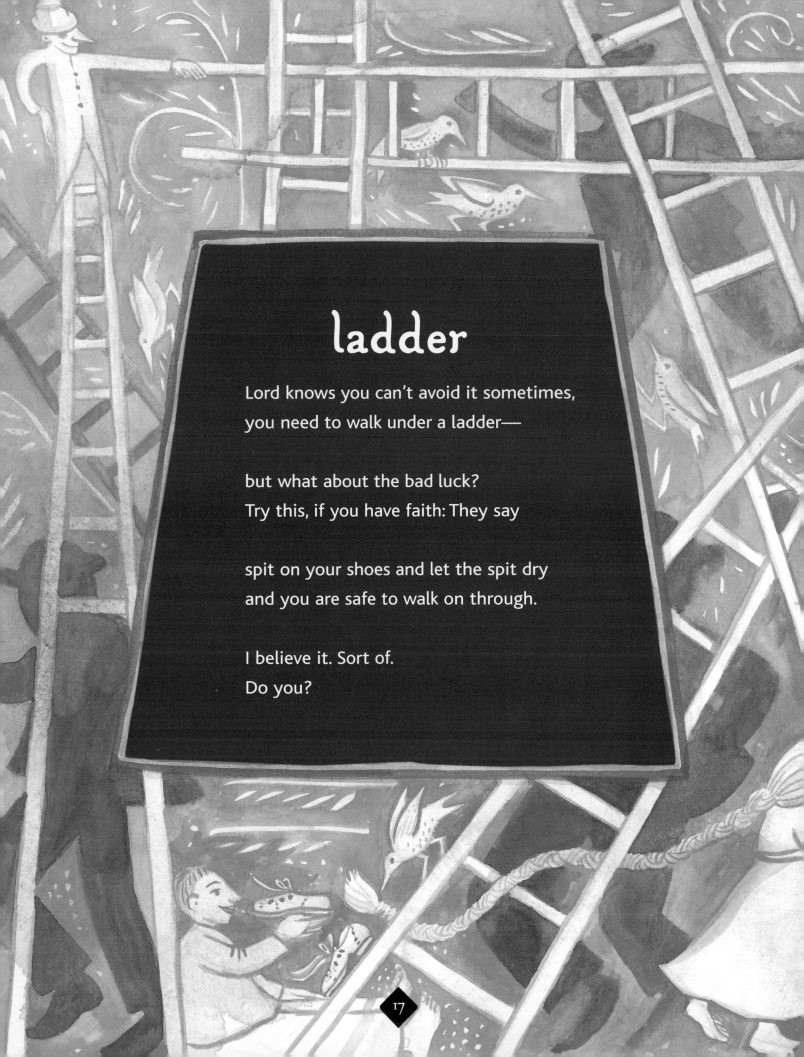

ladder

Lord knows you can't avoid it sometimes,
you need to walk under a ladder—

but what about the bad luck?
Try this, if you have faith: They say

spit on your shoes and let the spit dry
and you are safe to walk on through.

I believe it. Sort of.
Do you?

ladybug

Land on my hand for luck, ladybug.
Crawl all over my garden.

This is a safe place for your eggs.
I will watch your little black dragons grow.

I will tell them their mother was good.

mirror

The trick is to find sacred ground, the best you can.
Bring your broken mirror there,
here where the dirt is softer, dark.

Bury the pieces with a long straight arm.
Stop if you hear a dog's shrill bark;
fill the hole, start again,
who knows why.

Why the curse?

potatoes

Potatoes for your pocket, Granny.

Let them wrinkle for you, Granny.

Let them dry as hard as stones,

to pull the hurting from your bones.

rooster

The rooster crows
on the gate tonight.

The sky is turning.
Clouds are coming.

The wind blows through
his rooster crown.

Go home to your mom
in the close and
warm—

the rooster crows
how the wind will blow,

how the rain will roll
down the window.

salt

It is said

salt is magic. The pure kind, sea crystals.
Spilled salt is magic flung wild.

There is an antidote, an easy cure:
Throw a pinch of salt over your left shoulder.

For everything, you see, there is the reverse.

thirteen

Friday the 13th

thirteen witches are meeting in the Office of Bad Luck—
on the thirteenth floor at 13 Thirteenth Street, of course.

Zing! A boy falls off a horse and bites his tongue.
Zap! A tree at the zoo smashes a new car.
Zarg! A girl upchucks her lunch on the school bus floor—

and the witches are in stitches, laughing at us fools,
when the door slams
and the lights go out—

and thirteen unlucky witches have lost
their power.

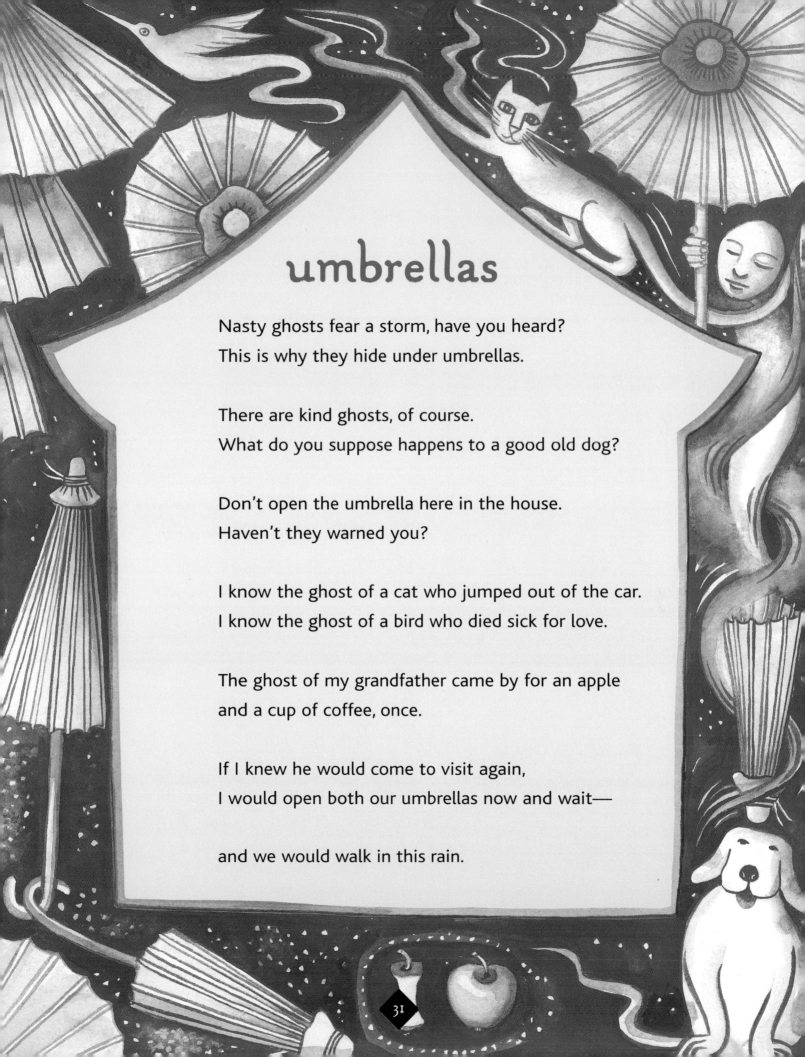

umbrellas

Nasty ghosts fear a storm, have you heard?
This is why they hide under umbrellas.

There are kind ghosts, of course.
What do you suppose happens to a good old dog?

Don't open the umbrella here in the house.
Haven't they warned you?

I know the ghost of a cat who jumped out of the car.
I know the ghost of a bird who died sick for love.

The ghost of my grandfather came by for an apple
and a cup of coffee, once.

If I knew he would come to visit again,
I would open both our umbrellas now and wait—

and we would walk in this rain.

wood

Spirits live in the trees,
different kinds—

oak for a mind whose grain runs deep,
pine for the soft-hearted,
cedar for the clear conscience.

They wait to serve you,
to seal your hopes with their sap,
to keep misfortune away.

Call on them
so your luck stays good:
Soul to soul,

knock on wood.

about the superstitions

CAT: Black cats were revered in Egypt, but feared in medieval Europe, where cat lovers marked them with the sign of the cross so they would not be associated with witches. Most Americans today think of black cats as unlucky. I heard of a man who walked backward for half a mile because a black cat crossed his path.

CLOVER: Apparently there is a legend saying that Eve stole a handful of clover from Paradise; for this reason, some think clover is magical.

EARS: If your ears itch, people supposedly are talking about you. I wonder: When my head itches, is someone thinking about me?

GARLIC: Garlic is considered a powerful talisman, warding off evil spirits, including vampires. I suspect that garlic has antibacterial or antiviral properties, which is why we eat it to battle a cold or the flu. It drives garden pests away, too, so you should plant some near your favorite flowers.

HAIR: There are tons of superstitions about hair—when to cut it, what to do with the clippings, why not to pluck white hairs, and more. I made up the one about standing bareheaded in the rain, so you might not want to try it.

HAT: I was surprised to learn that wearing your hat the wrong way could bring bad luck. Baseball catchers wear their hats backward—so maybe they should eat garlic, to be safe.

HORSESHOE: You should hang a horseshoe over a door, but how? Most prefer prongs up, to accumulate and keep their luck; some prefer prongs down, to sprinkle luck on those walking in and out.

KEYS: If you reach an intersection and don't know where to go, it is believed that the longest key in a bunch of keys, when the keys are tossed over your left shoulder, will point the way.

LADDER: The superstition against walking under ladders may have a religious connection. An open ladder could represent the Holy Trinity; walking under it (through the triangle) shows lack of respect for God. One variation allows a person to walk under after he spits on his shoes and lets the spit dry. Spitting on yourself shows humility, I guess; letting it dry shows patience.

LADYBUG: When a ladybug lands on you, you must not brush it off. The redder the bug, the better your luck!

MIRROR: If a broken mirror is like a broken spirit, burying the mirror lets the spirit rest and repair itself.

POTATOES: Potatoes are thought to cure rheumatism when they are carried in pockets and left to shrivel and harden. I would bet it is extra lucky if your potatoes sprout, and less lucky if they grow mold.

ROOSTER: If a rooster crows early in the evening, you can expect rain. This is a British superstition, and might not be quite as reliable in drier climates.

SALT: Some believe that salt over the left shoulder will cure any kind of bad luck, and they even carry salt in their pockets to use whenever needed.

THIRTEEN: There are many thoughts concerning the number thirteen, and some people consider it to be lucky. Many people consider it unlucky, though, so you will find buildings that skip a thirteenth floor. If I were in one of those buildings, I might feel nervous living or working on the fourteenth floor!

UMBRELLAS: Some people think an umbrella can be opened indoors as long as it is not held over your head. According to a Chinese superstition, however, ghosts live inside umbrellas, so they should never be opened indoors.

WOOD: Some people believe that guardian spirits live in trees. I would like to think that different kinds of spirits (with varying powers) live in different kinds of wood. This could explain why knocking on wood has not always worked for me.

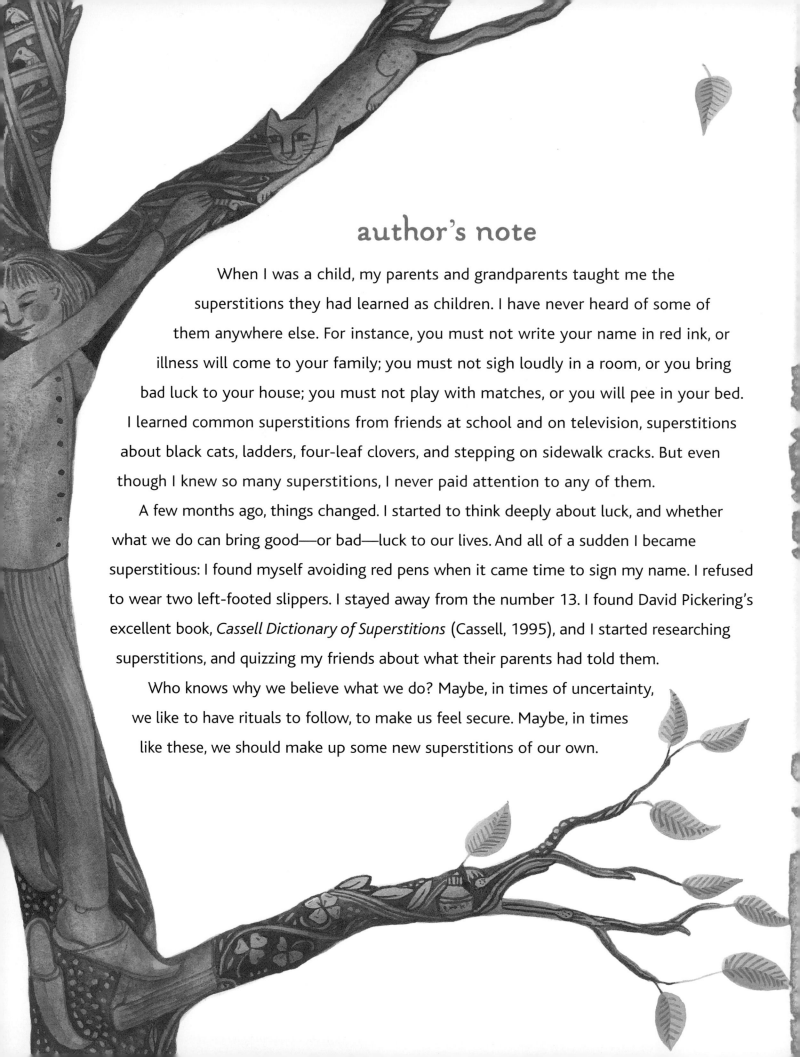

author's note

When I was a child, my parents and grandparents taught me the superstitions they had learned as children. I have never heard of some of them anywhere else. For instance, you must not write your name in red ink, or illness will come to your family; you must not sigh loudly in a room, or you bring bad luck to your house; you must not play with matches, or you will pee in your bed. I learned common superstitions from friends at school and on television, superstitions about black cats, ladders, four-leaf clovers, and stepping on sidewalk cracks. But even though I knew so many superstitions, I never paid attention to any of them.

A few months ago, things changed. I started to think deeply about luck, and whether what we do can bring good—or bad—luck to our lives. And all of a sudden I became superstitious: I found myself avoiding red pens when it came time to sign my name. I refused to wear two left-footed slippers. I stayed away from the number 13. I found David Pickering's excellent book, *Cassell Dictionary of Superstitions* (Cassell, 1995), and I started researching superstitions, and quizzing my friends about what their parents had told them.

Who knows why we believe what we do? Maybe, in times of uncertainty, we like to have rituals to follow, to make us feel secure. Maybe, in times like these, we should make up some new superstitions of our own.